LOAD 'ER UP
&
DRIVE SAFE

SHARING THE ROAD WITH BIG RIGS

STEVE GROVER

ISBN: 978-1-946203-32-8

Steve Grover
Grover Law Firm
Toll Free: 1 (877) 476-8379

Calgary:
Sovereign Centre Suite 390 – 6700 Macleod Trail SE
Calgary, Alberta T2H 0L3

Edmonton:
First Edmonton Place
Suite 587, 10665 Jasper Avenue
Edmonton, AB T5S 3S9

Expert Press

www.ExpertPress.net

Table of Contents

Dedication

This book is dedicated to the victims and the families
of the Humboldt tragedy.

Introduction

Imagine this: you're driving down the road, and you see a huge accident. The weather is cold. It's been snowing, and now the wind is picking it up, making almost blinding conditions so you can barely see what's up ahead.

Because of this, about ten vehicles have rear-ended each other. The Royal Canadian Mounted Police is out there, warning everyone to stop, which you do. But instead of staying in your car, you get out to see if anyone needs help.

All of a sudden, you see a semi-tractor trailer bearing down the road, and he's not slowing down. Maybe he's not paying attention; maybe the snow is blinding him. It doesn't matter. What matters is, he hits the 30 cars stopped behind yours. One of those cars, a Ford F150, hits you and sends you flying through the air into a snowbank.

It sounds like a horror story, but that story is true. It happened to one of my clients.

He was a former officer in the Canadian Navy, so his instincts, when he saw the crash, were to get out and help people. Because of that truck driver, however, those instincts ended up getting him severely injured. It also re-triggered his post-traumatic stress disorder, which came from his time in the first Gulf War in 1991.

Trucks fascinate us, and part of the reason they do is because of their incredible power. While they are useful and wonderful machines, when an accident happens involving a big semi-tractor trailer, especially one going fast with a full load, carnage is going to happen. Injuries are going to be far worse than an automobile accident. The damage to the vehicles involved is going to be far worse.

I don't want to imply that this fact makes trucks bad, quite the opposite. Trucks are great. They're a crucial part of our society. If it wasn't for truckers, I don't think commerce in North America would get done. We're so dependent on the highway and freeway system in Canada and America. Unlike other parts of the world that are more rail-focused, we simply couldn't survive without truckers.

If the truckers went on strike for a month, all the store shelves in your town would be empty of food. There would be no new clothes on hangers. There would be no gas at the gas station. The world as we know it would shut down.

Beyond our basic need for trucks and truckers, there's also something very iconic about them. They're a part of our culture and our history, as they should be, because it was truckers who helped build our country.

However, that does not mean that trucks aren't still dangerous and that they don't need to be held accountable. I know that almost first-hand, because a truck nearly kept me from ever existing in the first place.

My dad was a doctor, and when he was a young man interning at a hospital in England, a truck nearly killed him before he ever thought to have me.

It happened like this: he was on his way to work in the city. He was driving one of those little mini coopers because they were the popular vehicle to drive. Just ahead of him, there was a big rig with a big load strapped onto the back of its flatbed.

My father is a cautious driver, so he was following behind the rig at a safe distance. However, another vehicle was less patient and cut right in front of him. The next thing my dad saw was the load of the flatbed truck come down, hitch off the truck, and fall into the vehicle that had cut right in front of him. The person in that car died instantly. Afterward, it was discovered that the truck driver had not properly strapped down his load.

If my dad had been a little bit closer, or if that vehicle hadn't cut in front of him, I probably wouldn't have been here today. It's lucky for me that my father wasn't in that first car, but it's unfortunate it still happened to someone else, leaving a different family suffering.

My dad was a medical doctor, and there was nothing he could do in that situation. But I am a lawyer, and while I can't do anything about accidents that have already happened, I can help prevent future ones by fighting for the rights of those who have already been injured.

Because of the power lawyers have to help our clients, trucking companies have to take their responsibilities more seriously by following all the rules and regulations.

Statistics say about 62% of semi-tractor-trailers on the road in North America are not mechanically sound, which is quite a scary thought. Using the law is perhaps the best option we have to help change that statistic. We need to make sure truck drivers are properly trained and properly regulated. We need to make sure they keep their logbooks properly. We need to make sure drivers drive the correct number of hours, not deviating from a trip, not driving faster or taking shorter and fewer breaks than they're allowed. We need to make sure they're getting enough sleep. We also need to make sure that truck drivers are tested for alcohol and drug abuse. Because their responsibility on the road is higher than any automobile or motorcyclist out there, we need to make sure our trucks and truckers are safe.

In the big picture, I'm not against truckers. We all have to share the road, and we all want to get to work and get back home to our families and friends. In fact, this book is also for truckers. I hope they can pick up some practical information about what their obligation is on the road. And I hope they see that I respect them and their profession. They are central to our country's history and to its future. I just want to make sure we make trucks as safe as possible, and get compensation for those who were injured when they aren't.

So, to help both the casual drivers of cars and motorcycles as well as the professional truck drivers, this book has been designed to give an overview of what the trucking world looks like. Trucks are different from other vehicles in many ways, and it's important to understand what trucks are, how to drive safely with them on the road, and what to do if you ever are in an accident that involves one. In the coming pages, we will discuss all that and more.

By the way, ultimately, I did get that naval officer's case settled. He got the compensation he deserved, but that was an accident that could have easily been avoided if the truck driver had simply been more aware of his responsibilities and the power of the vehicle he was driving.

Chapter 1.

Living Behind the Wheel

People often think they understand what it's like to be a trucker. After all, truckers are all around us. As I said in the introduction, trucking is part of the culture in North America. We see them on the roads every day, and we see them on our TV screens and in movie theaters regularly as well.

On TV every week, you can watch *Ice Road Truckers*, where we learn about the truckers up in the Northwest Territories. Or, you could switch over to *Highway Thru Hell*, which follows truckers through the treacherous Coquihalla highway in British Columbia. There's also *Heavy Rescue 401*, which follows heavy recovery vehicles in Ontario.

Then there are the movies: *Smokey and the Bandit* with Burt Reynolds, *Over the Top* with Sylvester Stallone, and *Convoy* with Kris Kristofferson. Even Kurt Russell in *Big Trouble in Little China* was a rig driver.

These movies and shows provide us with some insight into what life behind the wheel is like, and they've been very successful doing it. However, these Hollywood productions really only show the exciting part of being a big rig driver. They show the side of trucking that, as a kid growing up, always made trucks fascinating to me. They're big, powerful, and full of cross-country adventure. Life for a trucker looks glamorous on TV and in the movies. The reality, though, is that truckers have a hard job and a hard life.

Nowadays, I respect truckers in large part not because of the glamorous side of their work but because they make their living doing a really hard job. Driving a rig all day long so we can all have food on our table is not an easy life. It keeps you away from your family. It can also be difficult on your health. Sitting so long, you're likely to develop back problems, and probably neck problems as well. The job is also at once stressful and quite monotonous. It can be difficult to make sure that you stay awake.

It takes a lot of skill to handle a big rig, and that requires a lot of training and qualifications. There are requirements for you and your vehicle that go well beyond anything you would see driving a motorcycle or a car.

To begin with, you have to take a commercial trucking test to qualify for a job. There are also specific qualifications, like an air brakes qualification. Then, there are qualifications required to transport certain cargo, such as hazardous materials like gasoline or toxic waste.

Beyond these qualifications, there are often specific regulations for different provinces or regions. In Canada, the Canadian Federal Regulations set a trucker's driving hours. The regulations stipulate that a trucker is allowed to do 13 hours of driving per day, with 14-hour maximum for on-duty time. After that, no driving is permitted. The driver has to take 10 hours off duty.

That may sound reasonable to you. The problem for truckers is the nature of their jobs. Truckers are regularly expected to do the impossible when hauling a load, making up time and distance that no one can do if they are following the rules.

Imagine you are a trucker, and your employer calls you up and says, "Hey, these goods have to get from Calgary to Vancouver in 8 hours." Well, technically, you can't get to Vancouver in 8 hours, because from Calgary to Vancouver it's a 10 hour drive. Unfortunately, sometimes these trucking companies put such unreasonable timeframes on their truckers because their concern is getting those goods across Canada or America, not the health and safety of their drivers.

To make that deadline, a driver is going to have to do something he shouldn't. He'll have to drive all night, drinking a bunch of caffeine and not breaking at all. Or, he'll have to speed the whole way, going far above the speed limit. Every time a trucker makes that choice, he is putting himself and others at risk.

Of course, taking those jobs is a choice that is up to the truckers. There are a lot of truckers I've met that just said, "Steve, I'm not going to drive for that company because they're completely unreasonable. They want me to get goods from Calgary to Edmonton in an hour-and-a-half, and I can't do it because it's a three hour drive. They'll pay me a bonus to get there, but I'm not going to put my health and my driving record at risk."

I find that attitude commendable, but I'm also sympathetic to the drivers and the trucking companies to some extent. No one wants to see empty shelves at Walmart right before Christmas. That's why the trucking companies press their truckers. No one wants to pass up a big bonus. That's why truckers agree to outrageous demands. The only way to keep those deals from happening is to regulate the industry or for lawyers like me to press forward with lawsuits when something goes wrong. That way, things have to be kept honest, and other solutions have to be found.

Perhaps, in this way, those TV shows do depict a certain amount of the difficulty in being a trucker. When we see a trucker driving on *Highway Thru Hell* in horrible road conditions, taking turns way too sharply, at a higher speed than he should, we can begin to see some of the struggles that come with the job. Not every trucker speeds down icy, twisty roads, but many truckers feel rushed on the job and make bad decisions on the road because of it.

That's an uncomfortably accurate portrayal of trucking, and it's the reason we need protections for everyone on the road in case something goes wrong.

Chapter 2.

Types of Trucks

Before we move any further along, I think it's important for us to discuss the different types of trucks out there. While most people only think of—and this book will often focus on—semi-tractor-trailers, the world of trucks is much vaster.

To start with, there are, obviously, those semi-tractor-trailers, the big rigs, also known as the 18-wheelers, although they may have more or fewer wheels. These trucks usually pull two trailers behind them.

Still, even here, there are so many different kinds of semi-tractor-trailers. For instance, there are ones that have an extended sleeper cab, where a trucker can relax, eat, and sleep. *

Others don't have that option.

Beyond the typical 18-wheeler, other large rigs include the flat bed truck, which has just the flat bed instead of trailers. Those can take loads like big tires.

Aside from the semi-tractor trailer, there are a number of large, specialized trucks. There are those that transport cars, where we see cars stacked in a double-decker formation. When it comes to transporting our gas, we get the big fuel trucks that carry oil after it's refined to the local gas station.

There are also refrigerated tractor-trailers that deliver frozen goods.

Now that we have cars, oil, and food, we need lumber for building our houses and furniture. So there's logging trucks for that.

For those who would rather move a whole house instead of new lumber, there are oversize loads hauled by big rigs. Those come with a whole crew of trucks, with a smaller truck ahead and another behind, telling everyone about the oversized load coming along.

You may also see commercial trucks that look like regular pickup trucks, but haul a long trailer with the tongue of the trailer in the back of the truck. These are many times referred to as "5th wheel" vehicles.

There are also huge garbage trucks that take care of both home garbage disposal and also those big garbage bins in the back of restaurants, apartment complexes, and shopping malls. And to help feed your hunger, there are many food trucks.

Moving on to the smaller trucks, we find a whole other set of services performed. We have delivery trucks, like FedEx and UPS, that usually deliver in big cargo van trucks.

We have smaller commercial trucks like auto parts trucks, which are usually Ford F-150s that have been registered as commercial vehicles. There are also plumbing vans and roofing company trucks. Like auto parts trucks, these vehicles are often non-commercial vehicles adapted to commercial use.

From transporting objects, we also need trucks that transport people. So, we have yellow school buses to take children to school every day. We also have commercial transportation like Greyhound and other tour buses.

And to transport our children to and from school, we always need to be aware of the standard school bus.

Emergency vehicles are also part of the trucking world. Ambulances and fire trucks are larger vehicles that have to be regulated, too.

As you can see, when you think of trucks in the big picture, we're not just talking about the big 18-wheelers like in *Smoky and the Bandit*. There are many other commercial vehicles that must be regulated and held accountable if they cause accidents. Drivers for these vehicles must be properly trained, whether they are delivering loads of lumber, cars, or plumbing supplies, or delivering children to school.

Chapter 3.

Different Standards

While all the vehicles in chapter 2 can be considered trucks, not all trucks and truck drivers are held to the same standards, although they all share some similarities.

To begin with, to operate any commercial vehicle, you must pass certain tests. While the tests and conditions required to drive a big rig are more stringent than for delivery trucks or construction trucks, all of them require preparation and testing.

In Alberta, for instance, a big rig driver would require a Class 1 license, which requires a normal, Class 5 license (for standard cars), passing a Class 1 knowledge-based test, passing a vision test and a physical, and submitting proof of an airbrake endorsement.

The Class 1 license is, as the name suggests, the highest class, allowing the holder to drive not just big rigs, but buses, taxis, ambulances, and vehicles with three or more axles. The only vehicle that can't be driven on a Class 1 license is a motorcycle.

For those looking to specifically drive a Greyhound or city bus, there is the Class 2 license, which has similar requirements, but with a Class 2 knowledge-based test.

For those who drive slightly smaller trucks, like dump trucks, a Class 3 license is required. Finally, for ambulances and school buses, a Class 4 license is mandatory.

Overall, truck drivers are held to a higher and more regulated standard than those driving a regular car. The obvious reason for this is that trucks are bigger, more powerful, and harder to manage. When you're driving a big rig, or even an ambulance, there are certain blind spots that you have because of the size of the vehicle. If you don't know how to accommodate your driving to those blindspots, serious accidents are likely to happen.

It's important to also know how to manage the weight of the load that you're carrying, the speeds you can go, and the number of gears that are required to shift down and shift up. A truck's transmission isn't as simple as a 6-speed standard auto vehicle.

The reason so much training, regulation, and testing is required is precisely because these vehicles are not as simple as cars. That makes the fact that 62% of the semi-tractor-trailers on the road are not mechanically sound even more frightening. If something finally breaks down, like the brakes, they could cause a lot of damage. The accidents when semi-trucks are involved are almost always big, the kind that leave a lot of injuries.

One of the major regulations that truckers have that is meant to prevent these accidents is the logbook.

These are required for certain commercial vehicle inspections done on trucks, and even F-150 trucks used by auto part shops.

A logbook tracks the hours you have been driving. As I mentioned above, semi-truck drivers have a set number of hours they can drive in a day. They have to have certain periods of rest. Logbooks allow authorities to track whether the driver has been complying with those requirements.

The layout, as you can see on the next page, is pretty straightforward. The logbook just shows your start time, where you started, your break time, where you took your break, and how many hours you drove. In theory, it paints a clear picture of what each day for the driver looked like, and it helps drivers avoid accidentally spending too many hours on the road.

Unfortunately, these can sometimes be forged, especially when there is pressure from trucking companies to make those impossible runs mentioned above. That can make it harder to hold drivers accountable, and it can take legal experts who know the trucking world to catch such faulty paperwork.

Thankfully, though, logbooks are now mostly digital, making it far harder to forge them.

Beyond logbooks, those who drive big trucks have other responsibilities as well. Those include stopping regularly at weigh stations.

You see weigh stations on the side of the road all the time. Trucks are expected to pull over to make sure the weight that they have is not

too heavy for the roadway. Weight is an important issue for trucks. It affects how quickly they can stop, as well as how easily they can turn and change lanes. If the weight is displaced in the wrong direction, it can throw off the truck's balance. In addition, trucks that are too heavy can tear up the roads quickly.

Provinces and territories take weigh stations seriously. If trucks haven't stopped at a weigh station, they can get pulled over and fined. Really, there's no excuse for skipping a weighing station anyway, unless a trucker is hiding something. These days, trucks don't even have to stop to be weighed. They just drive through and are weighed as they move.

The specifics of driving regulations are a province or state affair for the most part, although there is overarching federal oversight. If a truck stays in one province or state, that province or state will provide all the regulations for the truck. Once a truck crosses provincial or national borders, however, it must comply with federal standards. Here in Canada, Transport of Canada is the agency responsible for overseeing the trucking industry.

This provincial/federal divide extends to trucker insurance, which is significantly more expensive than regular driving insurance. In Alberta, drivers are required to have trucking insurance limits that cover at least $2,000,000 in damages and third-party liability. Often, they are part of umbrella policies of $5,000,000 or more.

However, once that truck leaves Alberta, even more insurance is required. If it's doing business in America, the law states that the truck has to carry an insurance policy that covers at least $5,000,000 in third-party damages.

I hope it is clear from these examples that trucks have vastly different standards from those of a normal car driver. They have to take additional tests and get special licenses. They come under special regulations and have to keep track of their time and movements. They have to be weighed regularly. And, they have to carry far more insurance.

All of this proves just how powerful trucks are. They are a valuable part of our economy and lives, but they are capable of causing great damage if they aren't regulated carefully. Making sure trucks are following these rules is part of my job.

Chapter 4.

How to Drive Safe

No matter what vehicle we drive, we all have to share the road. That includes you and me in our cars or on our motorcycles, the ambulance driver sitting in traffic, the fuel truck on the way to the corner gas station, and the big rig driver delivering goods from Calgary to Edmonton. We're all sharing the road together.

As automobile operators, we all have to respect the rules of the road to keep one another safe. That is especially true when it comes to trucks. More than at any other time, we have to be mindful of our driving. Otherwise, we could all end up in the same situation that my father witnessed in England, where a poorly secured load fell off and instantly killed the driver that was following too closely behind the truck.

With that story in mind, the first and most important lesson in driving safely around trucks is respecting the braking distance required for a tractor-trailer. If a tractor-trailer is going 100 km/h with a full load, and a Honda Civic is traveling beside it at the same speed, it could take twice as long for that tractor-trailer to come to a complete stop. Which makes sense, because the Honda Civic is a smaller and lighter vehicle. The force behind the truck is enormous, and so it can't stop nearly as quickly.

So, if you're driving, and all of a sudden, you're changing lanes in front of a semi-tractor trailer, respect the difficulty that trucker will have in trying to avoid hitting you at a short distance. Give them the room to slow down. If it's going 100 km/h, and then you cut in front of them at 90 or 100, that's a recipe for a major accident. That tractor-trailer could rear end you, and that would be your fault because he doesn't have enough braking distance to stop. The reaction time could be the same—maybe even a little faster since it is a professional tractor-trailer driver at the wheel—but given the load he's carrying and the speed he's going, it's going to take much more time and distance.

Another crucial point to consider is making sure every trucker sees us. Visibility is a major problem for truckers, and so we need to be sure not only that we see them, but that they see us. Trucks have a larger number of blind spots than cars do, and those blind spots are much bigger.

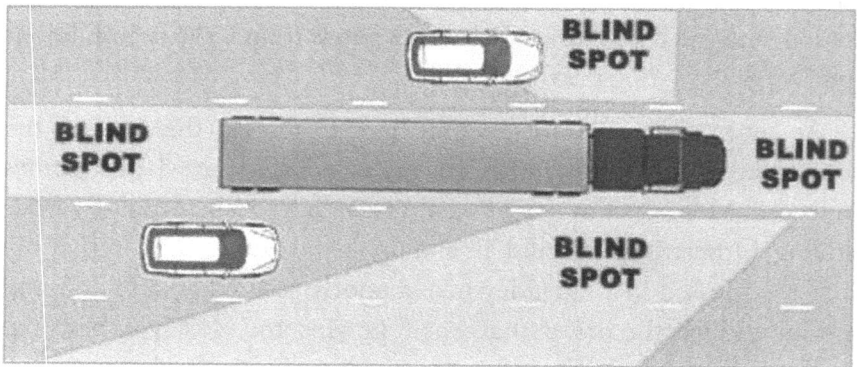

If your car is directly behind, directly in front, or directly beside a semi-truck, it is very likely that the truck driver can't see you. That means you have to be extra aware to make sure the truck doesn't begin switching lanes, slowing down, or speeding up without knowing you're there. Make every effort to move out of these blind spots as quickly as possible.

Finally, when it comes to cornering, it's important to remember that trucks need to slow down more and need more time and space to make a right-hand turn. While that process is quick and easy in a small vehicle, it can require a lot more maneuvering in a truck. Don't assume a truck is going to half-brake through a light and make a quick turn. Likewise, don't crowd a truck that may need to turn.

This all may sound like common sense to you. After all, most of us learn at an early age that not all vehicles are the same. All of this was likely in the driving manual you had to study to get your driver's license. But that doesn't mean we have really absorbed these facts. I know, early on in my life as a driver, that I hadn't. I remember when I was in my 20s. I was driving through Utah on the way to Los Angeles with my mom. I was going down Interstate 15, and I was cutting in front of tractor-trailers all over the road, weaving around them to get a little bit ahead and get a little more road behind me. Sure, I could hear that they were honking at me, but I didn't understand it.

It was at this point that my mom got me to pull over to the side of the road and said to me, "Listen, clearly Steve, you guys are going the same speed, and you just sped up a little bit. Then you cut in, changing lanes in front of a tractor-trailer, and then you slowed down. You're lucky he didn't rear end us. You have to respect truck drivers on the road. You could have gotten us killed back there."

That lesson has stuck with me ever since, and it is constantly reinforced by the cases I see where an accident has been caused by drivers simply not respecting each other and not giving each other the room necessary to drive safely.

I don't want to imply truck accidents are always the fault of car drivers and motorcyclists. In fact, it is usually the opposite. As we already know from earlier in the book, these accidents are often caused by truckers who are rushed or tired. Though they have a certain number of hours they can drive every day, some companies put pressure on truck drivers to break those rules in order to get deliveries to towns within certain unreasonable time limits. If a trucker agrees to that unreasonable time frame, obviously they are going to have to speed and speed excessively.

They may also have taken on more weight than is safe in their load. They want to get one or two more boxes of goods into that trailer, so they don't have to take it on a second run. If they aren't caught at a weigh station, they can end up being overweight, which makes it even harder to stop or control their truck.

There are also often drinking and drug problems that some drivers struggle with, which can make their driving erratic and unpredictable. Finally, there's always the risk of trucks simply breaking down.

All of this, though, only reinforces the above point: we have to respect other drivers and avoid driving aggressively around trucks. Even the safest truck driver will still struggle to slow down and to see everyone with all their blind spots. It's best to assume the truck in front of you on the road is not being handled by the safest truck driver. Which means, you should give every truck as much space as possible, in order to avoid accidents.

In the big picture, it's not only the responsibility of the trucker to drive properly, but also those of us in cars, on motorcycles, and even those of us riding bicycles.

We need to remember that the road isn't just ours. It belongs to everyone. It's the trucker's road too. We share it, and we share the responsibility of keeping each other safe.

Drive safely, and you are much less likely to ever need my services in the future.

Chapter 5.

What to Do if You Are in an Accident

No matter how much you take the lesson of chapter 4 to heart, and no matter how safely you drive overall, there is still always the risk you will be in a trucking accident. Unfortunately, accidents do happen in life, all the time, and they often involve commercial trucks. If you are unfortunate enough to be in an accident, and especially if you're injured, there are certain things that you need to do to protect yourself. That's true not only if you are a car operator or a motorcyclist, but also if you're a trucker or a big Greyhound bus driver.

In fact, no matter who you are or what you were driving, if you are in an accident, there are 8 steps you should follow every time.

- Check for injuries and call 9-1-1.

The first thing you should do is to check if you or anyone in your vehicle is injured. No matter what, call 9-1-1 right away and ask them to send the police. If someone is injured, request an ambulance. If you see fluid or debris on the roadway, request the fire department. Make sure the 9-1-1 operator knows how serious the accident is so they can properly respond to the accident

- Get the names and contact information of other drivers in the accident, but don't discuss the accident.

Get all the information you need from those involved in the accident. However, make sure you don't discuss the accident, and in particular, do not admit any guilt, even if you suspect you might be partly at fault. Usually, if a commercial truck is involved, supervisors, professional investigators, or even a lawyer from the trucking company will come out to the scene of the accident.

If you notice this, make sure that you note the names and phone numbers of all those representatives of the trucking company. The less you say to them or the trucker, the better. Ideally, it's best not to talk to them at all.

- Get the names and numbers of independent witnesses.

If there are independent witnesses, make sure you get their names and numbers. If they have business cards, take those. Make sure that when the police show up, the cop is aware there were independent witnesses.

- Take photographs of everything.

These days, everyone has a smartphone with them, so make sure you use yours.

Photographs are very important evidence. A picture, after all, is worth 1,000 words. So, take photos, as many as you possibly can. Take photos of your car from every angle, of tire marks and debris on the road, of other cars in the accident, and of the truck involved in the accident.

In addition to all that, make sure you take photos of your injuries and the injuries of those who were in the vehicle with you. Photograph any bruising, even if it seems minor. Sometimes, when people have a concussion, the only physical sign will be black eyes. If there are any cuts, any fractures, or any swelling, make sure you take pictures of that. With photographs, you can show that the accident was responsible for your injuries.

Visible signs of injury can fade faster than you realize, so be sure to take these photos early.

- Preserve any other evidence.

If you have ripped clothes or a part of your car or bike has fallen off, make sure you keep it or the police take it as evidence.

- Seek immediate medical treatment.

Whether you feel you are seriously injured or not, make sure you get medical treatment. If an ambulance arrives at the scene, be sure to get checked out by the ambulance attendants. If there is no ambulance, go to the hospital. You can't always be sure you haven't suffered a serious injury, and in such serious circumstances, it is always better to be safe than sorry.

- Contact your insurance company.

Once you've talked to the police and taken care of your medical needs, call your insurance company right away. Let them know that you've been in an accident. That includes both your auto insurance and your health insurance, if you have it. You have a duty to notify your insurance company of the accident and cooperate with them, so they can properly investigate the accident and protect your claims.

- Call a lawyer

This may seem like a dramatic step to some, but the truth is, in a serious accident, it is always good to have an experienced lawyer on your side as early as possible. This is, of course, something I know a great deal about, and I've seen the results of those who delayed too long in contacting a lawyer.

This topic is so important that I will leave it for the whole next chapter. For now, just recognize that the end result of an accident that involves a commercial vehicle may include the need for an experienced lawyer.

Following these steps is crucial to protecting yourself. An accident may only take an instant, but the ramifications can continue for years, and sometimes for a whole lifetime. Make sure you are prepared, no matter what the outcome of your accident is. Get the assistance you need at the scene and long afterward.

Chapter 6.

How and Why to Hire an Experienced Lawyer

In an ideal world, there wouldn't be much use for lawyers like me who specialize in motor vehicle accidents. Accidents, when they occurred, would be clear cut, and everyone would agree who was at fault. Those at fault would readily pay all damages, and life would go on.

Unfortunately, this isn't an ideal world. What I've found in doing a large number of tractor-trailer cases is that the trucker's job is often on the line any time they cause an accident. Too many accidents, or too severe an accident, and they'll get fired. They'll also get a bad driving record, which could make it hard to find another job.

All of this leads to an unfortunate fact: sometimes, truckers lie. Let me give you an example from one of my clients. Last year, this client was clearly rear-ended by a big semi-truck in Calgary. The cops decided it was a rear-end collision; the police report said it was a rear-end collision; the witnesses said it was a rear-end collision. However, my client went to the trucker's insurance company, and they said, "No, your vehicle cut off the truck. You made an improper lane change."

The trucking company and their insurance company took the trucker's story as the absolute truth, no matter what the witnesses and the cops said. Thankfully, after questioning, they admitted liability, and we were able to settle my client's case.

The truth is, often, careers and a lot of money are on the line in such accidents, and insurance companies, truck companies, and truckers want to sell the story that shows them least at fault. It's because of situations like that, which are unfortunately common, that you really need to bring an experienced lawyer in to protect your rights and set the story straight.

So, if you are in an accident, even if you are clearly, 100% not at fault, you could still struggle to prove it. In that situation, when you're already injured, you're already off work, and you're worried about bills and future income, you have to look to hire more than just any lawyer who will take your case.

After all, if you're going to purchase a house, even in a hurry, you're going to hire an experienced real estate lawyer to help you through the process. If, unfortunately, you and your spouse decide to get divorced, you're going to hire a lawyer that specializes in divorces and has experience handling divorces well.

That makes sense. You're not just going to hire a lawyer that does criminal law for your divorce because they won't know what to do. You wouldn't want to hire a divorce lawyer taking his first case either, if you could avoid it. What you obviously need from your lawyer in an accident case are two things: specialization and experience. So, if you're in a trucking accident, you want a lawyer like me, with years of experience and a specialization in truck-related accidents. Any other choice just hurts your case.

Don't make the mistake of assuming trucking cases are just like any other automotive case. Trucking accidents are very different from car accidents. First of all, they are usually way more severe, with way more damage involved. Unfortunately, the injuries are sometimes severely catastrophic. In other cases, they are fatal.

Beyond the severity of the accident, there's also a lot of investigating that has to go into looking into a trucking accident. To collect and interpret all the evidence in such cases, you need a lawyer that has the proper engineers and investigators available to get out there, go to the scene of the accident, and get the proof of who was at fault. These investigators take the time to talk to the investigating police officers who arrived on the scene, and they take the time to go down to the impound lot and look at all the vehicles involved.

These little steps can make all the difference in a case. One time, when I went down to the impound lot with one of my investigators, I found beer bottles in the sleep cabin of the rig. The trucker had been telling his company that he wasn't drinking. His story may have won out if we hadn't done more investigating. As it was, I was able to ask why he had a bunch of beer bottles in the back of his rig if he wasn't drinking. He eventually admitted under oath that he was drinking and that case settled.

There's so much that needs to be done to investigate the accident to make sure you're not found at fault, and not all of it is as simple as going and looking inside a truck. In a standard case, we hire investigators, accident reconstructionists, and engineers to go out to where the accident took place and completely reconstruct the scene, so we can figure out exactly how the accident happened. This process involves taking measurements and looking for debris that may still be on the roadway. It involves looking for skid marks and other tire marks so they can gauge braking distances.

Then, other experts take the black box from all the vehicles involved in the accident and interpret the data to get an even clearer picture of what happened.

These investigations are often time sensitive, which means it's important to contact an experienced lawyer early so they can send experts out to collect all possible data. Cities in North America are changing every day at an incredible pace. Cars drive over evidence and carry it away. The weather also erases evidence. The rain, the snow, and the wind come down and erode tire marks or blow debris away. Then, cities may have to change the road, laying new asphalt on top of evidence or redirecting the road. Within a few months of the accident, that whole intersection where your accident took place could be changed, at which point there would be much less evidence for your case.

I remember one particular case in which I was very glad we were contacted early. One night, while I was on that case, I happened to be driving through the intersection where the accident happened after dinner. It actually took me a moment to realize it was the right place. I'd seen all the photos, but as I looked at it now, that intersection had already completely changed. The client had hired me less than six months before.

It isn't just the roads that can change, either. Sometimes, witnesses disappear. There could be a key witness to your case who could move out of the area or pass away. If you don't have a lawyer there to get your evidence recorded and organized early, you can discover your case has fallen apart overnight sometimes.

Then, on top of the rapidly disappearing evidence, you still have to contend with that trucker, the trucking company, and the insurance company. The thing with trucking cases is there are huge insurance policies involved. Because of the personal and corporate financial pressure, truckers sometimes change their story, making it even harder to corroborate and prove definitively what happened. Insurance companies also know how much money is on the line as well, and they will often decide, "We're not just going to settle this out. We're going to fight it tooth and nail. No matter what." They want to see if you'll blink first and back down.

As you can see, accident cases that involve trucks can be complex. Thankfully, a lawyer who specializes in this area, like myself, will be familiar with the whole process and already know what type of tricks to expect and what type of evidence you need. However, if you don't hire the right lawyer, one that knows all the ins and outs of a case like this, you could lose out on a lot. The wrong lawyer could settle the case for a very small amount when your case is worth a hundred times more. Or, they might even lose the case outright.

Knowing that, you should hire a lawyer that is willing to not only investigate the accident, but prove definitively how the accident occurred. You need a lawyer that is willing to fight until you are offered a fair settlement. Your lawyer should have experts on hand to prove your damages for injuries and financial losses. Just as important, though, is that your lawyer has the stamina and the fight to continue to take on your case for years and years, if need be, knowing that the insurance company is not just going to write you a check one day without testing your resolve.

So, if you're taking the time to go see all the right doctors about your injuries and taking the time to go to all your physiotherapy appointments with specialists, take the time to ask around to find the right lawyer to deal with your case. Don't settle for just any injury lawyer, find a trucking accident lawyer who knows the law and has the experience to handle anything a trucker, trucking company, or insurance company might throw at them.

Do some research, and I'm confident that if you're in my area, you'll find that I can do the best work for you. I deal with these cases every year, and I know what it takes to get you the compensation you deserve. If you have any questions, feel free to contact me, so we can start helping you today.

Chapter 7.

Types of Damages

Let's say, unfortunately, you were injured in the accident, and you've decide you are going to bring a claim. You've gone out and you're looking into hiring a lawyer who has dealt with trucking accident cases and who knows how to properly litigate your case. Now, the question arises, what kind of damages are you entitled to due to your injury?

To begin with, in Canada, you have a legal right to sue somebody if you've been wronged and injured. If you win your case (or settle), you are entitled to compensation for a number of different types of damages.

It's important to point out here that how much compensation you can earn depends on which province (or American state) the accident occurred in. For the purposes of this chapter, I will focus generally on Alberta, where my practice is located. If you want to know more specifics about your area, you should contact a local accident lawyer to find out more.

Now, the types of damages you can receive compensation for after a trucking accident are:

* Pain and suffering

A figure is arrived at based off of how much pain and suffering you have and will go through. That number can cover a wide spectrum, depending on a judgment for how much pain you are likely to continue to experience indefinitely. However, in Canada, there is a cap on how much can be awarded for this particular type of damages, which currently is $370,000.

- Loss of income

If you're off work, you're entitled to get your past loss of income back. Past loss of income awards a person for the income that he or she has lost from the date of the accident to the date of settlement or judgement of the trial of the case. In Alberta, that is based on your net loss of income, not on your gross income. Essentially, you calculate what your net income is by deducting about 25% off your gross. If you have lost out on $10,000 gross, for instance, you're entitled to about $7,500.

- Loss of future income/Loss of earning capacity

If your injuries are going to affect your ability to work in the future, you can receive compensation. If you can't work at all, you can make a claim for future lost income. Alternatively, if you can work but only at a diminished level, you can claim for lost earning capacity. For instance, say you used to work construction and now you can't do heavy lifting like before the accident. However, you can still work and make a living, you are just confined to sedentary light duty jobs. In that case, you can make a claim for loss of earning capacity.

It is important to note that you can't recover future loss of income and lost earning capacity. It's only one or the other.

- Special damages

Another type of damages that you can be awarded are for your out-of-pocket expenses incurred due to the accident. After an accident, you have to go to the doctor. You have to visit your lawyers. You have parking expenses, travel expenses. You buy Advil, Tylenol, heating pads, and ice packs. You buy yourself a special ergonomic chair. If your doctor recommends a purchase, keep the receipts. If your insurance companies don't cover it, you can recover these expenses through special damages.

* Past and future loss of housekeeping

If your ability to complete housekeeping chores has been affected by your accident, you can be compensated for the need to hire outside help. If you can no longer do any cooking, cleaning, or laundry, or even if it just takes you longer to do it, you can make a claim for past and future housekeeping.

* Future cost of care

Unfortunately, some injuries don't ever completely heal. If your accident leaves you with a brain injury, psychological issues that require ongoing treatment, or chronic pain that requires treatment by a physiotherapist, massage therapist, or chiropractor, you can receive compensation.

* Punitive damages

Punitive damages come into play when the trucker, the trucking company, or the insurance company has acted in a malicious, oppressive, or high-handed fashion that offends the court's sense of decency. Unfortunately, in Canada, unlike America, it's a relatively high bar to meet, but it is becoming more common.

In trucking cases, punitive damages can come into play when a trucking company tells their truckers to drive at high speeds, or when they know that a driver was not properly regulated to drive a truck. They may also be required to pay if they knew that their driver had a history of getting high or drinking alcohol all the time while driving and never took any steps to get him off the road.

To finish this chapter up, I'd like to discuss a major concern for many who are considering filing a lawsuit: contingency fees. The question always arises in these situations, "how much is it going to cost me to hire a lawyer?" The answer is that contingency fees make sure you don't pay anything. Until you win, I work for free. If you come to my office and we pursue a case today, I finance the whole file, and I hire all the experts to investigate the accident. The expenses I incur to litigate your case, called disbursements, will be reimbursed to my office on top of your settlement.

If you win, then I charge a flat 30%, which comes out of your settlement. I don't send you any bills in the interim, and if the case doesn't bring a settlement, I don't make a penny. So, if the potential cost of a lawyer is keeping you from seeking compensation after your trucking accident, stop worrying about the costs. You'll never see a bill until after you win, so there's no reason to avoid going to a lawyer any longer.

Chapter 8.

A Case I Settled

To help illustrate how a trucking lawsuit works, I want to end this book with an example case from my own experience. For the sake of all those involved, I've changed the names.

My client, who I will call Joe, was leaving work after doing a night shift for a food distribution company in Calgary. It was early morning in the winter, and it was snowing. He was driving through an intersection, and a big truck for XYZ Trucking Company made an illegal left turn in front of his vehicle, which left him pinned under the front part of the semi-tractor trailer. Ambulance and fire department were called. The jaws of life were required to get him out of his car.

When they got him to the hospital, he was diagnosed with a brain injury. A CT scan and MRI found damage to his frontal lobe area, which affected Joe's ability to do multi-tasking jobs. He was also suffering from chronic pain and had many cognitive and psychological issues. His memory was affected. He was forgetful. He also struggled with socializing.

As you can imagine, that had a very serious effect on his life. Joe wasn't able to go back to his food distribution job because he couldn't multi-task anymore. Instead, he ended up shelving stock at a supermarket. He was making less money than before the accident. In addition, he was advised by the doctors not to drive anymore, which further limited his ability to find better work.

Partly due to all these issues, he and his wife, Sally, got separated during the course of the case. However, since Joe and his family didn't have enough money, he couldn't move out. He had to move into the basement of the house, while Sally and their two children lived up on the main level. It was an intolerable situation, but they had no other options at that time.

When Joe contacted me and told me his story, I told him he had a clear case, and we decided to sue the trucking company. We went out and got our accident reconstructionists and engineers to reconstruct the accident, take photos of the scene, inspect the tractor-trailer that hit my client and inspect his vehicle, which was written off. Then, we looked into the situation with the truck driver. It turned out that the defendant driver of the XYZ Trucking was charged with a wrong left turn by the Calgary Police Service. He was later convicted of the charge, although he refused to come to my office to be questioned.

We also questioned some corporate defendants of the trucking company. They had very few documents about the accident. There are certain things that they should've done in their investigation that they didn't do. A lot of their records were not there. We also spoke with medical experts to prove my client's injuries.

Despite the evidence of fault on the part of their truck driver and the clear impact of the accident, however, XYZ Trucking didn't initially take the case seriously. They offered me a nominal amount to settle the case before we started our lawsuit. Considering how much Joe was suffering, it was an insulting figure. So, we started the process of going to court.

That process, however, was purposefully slowed down. One common tactic sometimes used by insurance companies or trucking companies is denying the claim. They'll defend themselves even when their argument is absurd, and they'll delay proceedings as long as possible, hoping that the plaintiff becomes exhausted or even dies. Not all insurance companies are that way, but some are. Joe's case, unfortunately, involved one of the bad ones, and it took eight years from the date of the accident to reach the date of settlement.

This insurance company's tactic was to bring in a new lawyer for the case every year. That meant, every year, they had to come up to speed with what was going on in the case, which caused enormous delays.

Finally, though, with the eighth lawyer on the case, in the eighth year of the case, we did set a five-week trial date. Only at that point did they finally take the case seriously, hiring their own investigators to see how the accident happened, and hiring their own medical expert to dispute my client's brain injury.

Before the trial, the lawyer for the insurance company agreed to mediation, which is a joint meeting with both parties in the lawsuit, using a mediator, who is a neutral third-party. This individual tries to facilitate a settlement between the two parties. The point is to try to resolve the case before a trial, to the satisfaction of all parties.

The mediation took a whole day. The senior adjustor for the insurance company flew out to the mediation from Toronto. Amazingly, once they became intimately aware of the situation and actually met with Joe and Sally, the insurance company decided to settle not for what we expected, but for much more. In fact, Joe received an almost seven-figure settlement. After eight years, he was finally able to move on with his life, with the money he needed to start over.

After the claim was resolved, Joe and Sally were finally able to file for divorce and live their separate lives. Joe now works full-time, not to the capacity he was before the accident, but at the level he's capable, and the settlement money continues to supplement his income. He's been careful with the settlement money, investing some of it to make sure it will last.

He has also learned to adapt to his limitations. He now uses pads of paper, sticky notes, and his iPad to remind himself to do things like taking out the garbage on Tuesday or doing laundry on Sunday.

Though it was a long time coming and a tremendous amount of work, both Joe and I were very satisfied with the resolution of the case. Joe was provided with the money and the closure to move on, and I was happy to close the file and consider it a job well done.

I hope this story illustrates just how important it is to hire the right lawyer if you're going to take on a trucking company. Joe's case was fairly clear cut, and it still took years and a lot of dedication on the part of our law firm. If you're looking for a lawyer to represent you in a trucking case like Joe's, you have to find one who understands trucking cases through and through, one who knows how to present your case and to quantify the damages you have suffered due to the accident. And you especially need one who understands how to be proactive on your case.

Insurance companies don't just write checks. You have to prove your injuries and your losses to the insurance company and the court. You have to have all your ducks in a row and have your experts there to confirm who was at fault and to prove your damages claims. While it is true that most cases are settled, and most don't take nearly as long as Joe's, you still need to make sure that you have a lawyer who is ready to go to trial, if it comes to that. Your lawyer should live by the words Sun Tzu said in *The Art of War*: "If you want peace, prepare for war."

Taking on Joe's case was very frustrating. It was a lot of work, but looking back on it now, it was very satisfactory work. We did a good job for Joe. The amount of money he got was fair and reasonable, and when I recently touched base with him, he seemed happy. If you've been injured in a trucking accident, I hope I can help you and provide that same kind of fair and reasonable resolution for you.

Conclusion

I want to thank you for taking the time to read my book. I hope it was as enjoyable to read as it was to write. This is my second book, the first being *Ride Hard, Ride Safe*, which was about motorcycles and motorcycle accidents. Both these topics are very close to my heart.

I believe everyone can benefit from reading this book, because a large part of our society drive as their main source of transportation. Roadways and highways are our lifeline, and trucks are part of that experience.

Hopefully, car and truck drivers both find this book useful. After all, we all have to share the road together. I believe trucking companies and truckers are a vital part of our society. I respect the job they're doing. I know it's a hard job. It's rewarding for them, but it's also a job with a high level of responsibility. Their decisions affect lives, and they can cause a lot of damage if they aren't careful.

With this book, I hope truckers will be inspired to continue to take their jobs seriously. I want them to make sure that their trucks and trailers are mechanically sound, to take the time to get enough rest, to take care of their brakes as required by law, and to get the proper qualifications.

Most important to me, though, is that we all, collectively, make the highway safer, so we can all get where we're going without anyone getting hurt. We see injured people in our office every day, and if this book can help avoid just one accident from happening, one accident like the one that affected Joe or the one that nearly affected my father, I feel I've done my job.

If you or your family have been involved in an accident involving a tractor-trailer, please feel free to reach out to me to ask me any questions. You can contact my office to book an appointment with myself or one of my lawyers. If you just want to learn more about my law firm and what type of work we do, please feel free to visit our website at groverlawfirm.com for more information.

Thank you again.

About the Author

Steve Grover was born and raised in Calgary, Canada. For almost 20 years, he has worked as a personal lawyer, protecting those injured in accidents. His focus is on injury cases involving brain injuries, catastrophic claims, and wrongful death involving trucking accidents. He's passionate about his work, and he cares about doing well for his clients. He is a member of the Academy of Truck Accident Attorneys (ATAA).

In May 2017, he was asked to share his expertise at the APITLA National Interstate Trucking Super Summit in Tampa Bay, Tampa, Florida. There, he informed the audience about a range of topics related to trucking accidents in Canada.

Copies of his book are available for free in his office, online, or at public events. To be added to the mailing list for his firm's free bimonthly newsletter, contact his office.

www.ingramcontent.com/pod-product-compliance
Lightning Source LLC
Chambersburg PA
CBHW071336200326
41520CB00013B/3000